Microgreens

A Complete Step by Step Beginners Guide for Growing Microgreens

Basil Green

Download the Audio Version of This Book FREE

This book is best enjoyed in its audio format! If you love listening to audio books on-the-go, I have great news for you. You can download the audio book version of this book for **FREE** just by signing up for a **FREE** 30-day audible trial! See below for more details!

Audible trial benefits

As an audible customer, you'll receive the below benefits with you 30-day free trial:

- Free audible copy of this book

- After the trial, you will get 1 credit each month to use on any audiobook

- Your credits automatically roll over to the next month if you don't use them

- Choose from over 400,000 titles

- Listen anywhere with the audible app across multiple devices

- Make easy, no hassle exchanges of any audiobook you don't love

- Keep your audiobooks forever, even if you cancel your membership

- And much more

Go to the links below to get started

FOR AUDIBLE US:

bit.ly/microgreensfree

FOR AUDIBLE UK:

bit.ly/microgreensfreeuk

© Copyright 2020 - All rights reserved.

The content contained within this book may not be reproduced, duplicated or transmitted without direct written permission from the author or the publisher.

Under no circumstances will any blame or legal responsibility be held against the publisher, or author, for any damages, reparation, or monetary loss due to the information contained within this book, either directly or indirectly.

Legal Notice:

This book is copyright protected. It is only for personal use. You cannot amend, distribute, sell, use, quote or paraphrase any part, or the content within this book, without the consent of the author or publisher.

Disclaimer Notice:

Please note the information contained within this document is for educational and entertainment purposes only. All effort has been executed to present accurate, up to date, reliable, complete information. No warranties of any kind are declared or implied. Readers acknowledge that the author is not engaged in the rendering of legal, financial, medical or professional advice. The content within this book has been derived from various sources. Please consult a licensed professional before attempting any techniques outlined in this book.

By reading this document, the reader agrees that under no circumstances is the author responsible for any losses, direct or indirect, that are incurred as a result of the use of the information contained within this document, including, but not limited to, errors, omissions, or inaccuracies.

Table of Contents

Table of Contents..5

Introduction..1

Chapter 1...2

What Are Microgreens?..2

    The Popularity of Microgreens.....................................2

    The Structure of Microgreens.......................................3

    Terminology..3

    How Nutritious Are Microgreens?................................4

Chapter 2..6

Tips for Growing Microgreens...6

    Is Microgreen Consumption Risky?..............................9

    Introducing Microgreen into Your Food....................10

Chapter 3..13

Types of Microgreens..13

        Arugula...13

        Asparagus..14

        Barley..14

        Basil...15

        Beets..15

        Broccoli...16

        Buckwheat..16

        Cabbage..17

        Carrot..17

        Cauliflower...17

- Celosia 18
- Chervil 18
- Corn 18
- Endive 19
- Lettuce 19
- Mustard 20
- Radish 20

Differences Between Microgreens and Baby Greens 20
Popular Microgreens and Their Nutritional Value 21

Chapter 4 23
Microgreen Troubleshooting Tips 23
- Mold 23
  - Troubleshooting Mold 24
- Fallen Greens 25
  - Troubleshooting Fallen Greens 25
- Yellow Microgreens 26
  - Troubleshooting Yellow Microgreens 26
- Clumped Greens 26
  - Troubleshooting Clumped Greens 27
- Slow Germination Time 27
  - Troubleshooting Slow Germination Time 27

Chapter 5 29
How to Grow Microgreens at Home 29
- Cultivating Your Microgreens 29
- Benefits of Growing Microgreens 30

Chapter 6 33
Health Benefits of Eating Microgreens 33

Chapter 7 36

Some Microgreen FAQs 36

Chapter 8 48

Some Microgreen Recipes 48

    Beef Burger 48

    Parmesan and Ricotta Cheese Pizza with Microgreens 50

    Sunflower Guacamole 51

    Mini Strawberry Chocolate Tart 52

    Sheet Pan Fajitas with Bell Peppers and Chickpeas 53

    End of Summer Salad 54

    Bacon Hash Brown Casserole with Eggs 56

    Microgreens with Strawberry-Lime Vinaigrette 57

    Lemon and Pea Tendril Risotto 58

    Mediterranean Quinoa Salad 60

    Charred Rainbow Beet and Pistachio Salad 61

    Roasted Broccoli Microgreen Soup 62

    Mushroom and Microgreen Omelet 63

    Asparagus, Tomato, and Microgreen Salad 64

    Kale and Radish Microgreen Salad 65

    Seared Sea Scallops with Microgreen Salad 67

    Seared Halibut with Microgreens Salad 68

    Microgreen, Zucchini, and Carrot Cake 69

    Super Microgreen Smoothie 70

    Blue Cheese Tomato with Microgreens 71

    Cold Smoked Salmon Sandwiches with Microgreens 72

    Vegan Microgreen Soup 72

Conclusion 75

References 76

Bonus! 77

Before We Begin…

If you enjoy this book then I'd like to ask you for a favor. Would you be kind enough to **leave a review for this book on Amazon?**

It'd be greatly appreciated & will likely help other avid green thumbs with their projects! I read EVERY review I receive and each one helps me to serve each and every one of you better, so your feedback is highly valued!

Thank you,

Basil Green

Introduction

Microgreens are often no bigger than 3 inches in height. They are quite young (no more than seedlings) but do not mistake that for being less nutritious. In fact, these young greens usually contain more nutrients than their more mature vegetable counterparts. And this is one reason why a lot of individuals choose them.

The aroma they bring to any dish and their rich healthy colors make for beautiful garnishes. Their high nutrient content and beautiful aesthetic might be why you've chosen to learn more about microgreens. Or perhaps you are a gardner who wishes to learn how to grow healthy microgreens. Maybe you even want to learn about both.

Whichever the case, you're reading the right book. Everything from the correct conditions for successfully cultivating microgreens to recipes made with them will be treated in this book. It also doesn't matter how much or little you know about microgreens, you're covered.

Since you're interested in microgreens, prepare yourself. This will be the most profitable and enjoyable book you've read all year. Let's get to it now.

Chapter 1

What Are Microgreens?

Microgreens is a term used to describe aromatic greens otherwise known as vegetable confetti or micro herbs, which have rich flavors and introduce a splash of color in various dishes. Regardless of their relatively small size, microgreens have rich nutritional values, making them a healthy component in any food. Microgreens typically exist as young vegetable greens with a height range of one to three inches, or 2.5 to 7.5 centimeters, including their stem and leaves. Their height range puts them in a similar class to baby greens, sprouts, and shoots, but they are a distinct category and can be classified as the stage between sprouts and baby greens. They are smaller than baby greens like radicchio, arugula, spinach, et cetera, but are harvested earlier after the sprout stage.

The distinction further widens as sprouts have a shorter growing cycle, ranging from 2 to 7 days. Microgreens, on the other hand, are typically ready for harvest between 7 to 21 days after they germinate. That is, microgreens are formed after the development of cotyledon leaves. Harvesting is done by cutting the stem just above the soil line.

The Popularity of Microgreens

Microgreens are typically purchased or grown by people with an eye for nutrition. Otherwise, they are used for their ability to lend aesthetic and flavor to food, especially by fine dining outlets. Chefs typically use microgreens for their ability to lend color while improving the taste and attractiveness of several dishes by capitalizing on their unique delicate textures and distinct flavors like spicy and sweet.

Microgreens are grown from a variety of herbs, vegetables, and other plants, and have been a regular show on the menus of chefs stretching back into the '80s in San Francisco. In the mid-90s, growing microgreens became popular in Southern California and the tradition has continued. Initially, only very few varieties of microgreens were used. Among them were kale, basil, cilantro, arugula, beets, as well as a colorful mix of those known as "Rainbow Mix." As they grew in popularity, microgreens spread to the east from California, reaching many areas in the United States where they are now grown in many varieties. In recent times, the industry for microgreens has expanded to involve several different growers and seed companies.

The Structure of Microgreens

There are three main parts common to all microgreens, namely a cotyledon leaf, a central stem, and the first pair of young true leaves. The size of microgreens differs, but the average size typically lies within the 1 to 1.5 range (2.5 to 3.8 cm). While this is the range in which a plant qualifies to be called a microgreen, some exceed this range and are regarded as petite greens. Microgreens have a life cycle of 2 to 4 weeks from seedling to harvest.

Terminology

In the true sense of the word, microgreens isn't a real word with any scientific history and is merely a construct of marketing terminology. Like "baby greens" which conceptualizes their stages of development. Conversely, the term sprouts refers to germinated seeds, which are usually eaten whole, including the shoot, seed, and roots, based on the variety.

For instance, sprouts of plants like peanuts, pumpkins, and almonds tend to have more preferable flavors when harvested earlier.

How Nutritious Are Microgreens?

In early 2014, publications from the USDA Agricultural Research Service's researchers boasted of a variety of studies that describe the nutritional value of microgreens. These studies also include vital information like their shelf life and growth cycle. According to the studies in these publications, about 25 varieties of microgreens were examined and their main nutrients measured. Among these nutrients are vitamin E (tocopherols, vitamin K (phylloquinone), vitamin C (ascorbic acid), a precursor to vitamin A (beta-carotene), among other affiliated carotenoids.

Of the 25 samples of microgreens used in the study, garnet amaranth had the highest concentration of vitamin K; red cabbage vitamin C; green daikon radish vitamin E; and cilantro carotenoids. On a general note, microgreens had higher levels of carotenoids and higher vitamin concentration (up to five times greater) than their average mature plant counterparts. This implies that microgreens may well be worth the hype and trouble of growing and delivering them fresh within their short life cycle.

In 2012, a summertime nutritional study conducted by the University of Maryland's Department of Nutrition and Food Science showed promising results implying that microgreens could contain high nutritional content in comparison to other mature veggies. At Texas A&M University, a director of the Vegetable and Fruit Improvement Center and horticulture professor, Bhimu Patil agreed on the potential of microgreens to have higher nutritional values than their mature vegetable counterparts. However, he noted that more studies would be necessary for side-by-side comparison between both varieties. While he agrees on nutrient composition, Patil is wary that discrepancies could exist in nutritional value based on factors such as the soil medium, time of harvest, and place of planting.

According to researchers from the above mentioned studies, the best and most nutritious microgreens are those that have higher color intensities. Although the nutritional value may vary across microgreens, many varieties tend to have high copper, zinc, potassium, magnesium, and iron content. Among their beneficial constituents are antioxidants which are helpful in boosting the immune system. Given their high nutrient density, microgreens have higher levels of antioxidants, minerals, and vitamins than an equal amount of their mature counterparts. However, this doesn't necessarily prove that this quality is constant across all varieties of microgreens.

Chapter 2

Tips for Growing Microgreens

1. **Proper timing is everything**: Wherever you live, whether it's cold, hot, or temperate, chances are you can cultivate some variety of microgreens some time of year outdoors or indoors. A key factor to successfully growing and harvesting microgreens is planning your time right. Planting your seed during the wrong time period will only render your resources and efforts useless. Microgreens ought to be cultivated within a short period of one to three weeks and consumed quickly for an optimal outcome.

   As such, cultivation in the right season is imperative. Some varieties require warmer climates for germination, while some may favor colder weather. Delve into planting only after carrying out your research, and pick the best time of year for your planting season. One handy lesson is to keep an age-old farming practice in mind. This logic requires growing crops in alignment with the different phases of the moon every other month.

   You will find it astonishing to know that the moon has a gravitational pull effect, which not only affects tides, but the flow of plant sap and soil moisture as well. In this light, sowing your microgreens during these periods will ensure optimal absorption of moisture and nutrients, resulting in faster growth and germination cycles.

   While seemingly trivial, this logic makes a huge difference in speeding up the cultivation of healthy "fast food" for domestic or commercial purposes. If you are worried about missing the moon's phases, you could try getting a moon calendar. They are usually sustainable, easy to use, and are applicable around the world, despite variations in climate and time zones.

2. **Protecting your plants is key**: Just like any other thing you hold dear, your plants require shelter, not only to be shielded from harsh weather conditions but from other factors as well. For microgreens grown outside, they will be exposed to other factors that might prey on them. Birds, rodents, and ants feast on seeds, so microgreens are a snack in their eyes. Hence, you need to protect your microgreen seeds until germination. Nothing fancy, just go DIY on this tip. Try using clear lids, plastic bags, upcycled bottles, or a mini greenhouse. Doing this can help create a humid environment for proper seed germination.

3. **Prevent the formation of mold**: Mold is a killer of microgreens and should be avoided at all costs. It is particularly a problem for people living in warmer climates. The humid weather in subtopic regions aid the formation of mold, so it can quickly become a problem.

   A fan can come in handy in boosting air circulation. Most microgreens will prefer a relative humidity of 40 to 60 percent, but this can vary between plants. Also, only sowing a few seeds in a single pot or tray can help with aeration and nutrient intake, as there won't be much competition among the plants.

4. **Go easy on your microgreens:** Think of microgreens as the toddler stage in plant life, keep in mind their fragile leaves and stems which could so easily get damaged. Endeavor to treat them delicately when handling. Rather than spray with a watering can, try misting with a spray can or watering from the bottom up. Handling techniques can also vary across microgreen variety, as they exhibit different characteristics during growth. Some tend to

grow short and straight, like rocket or basil, while others turn out quite tall, like buckwheat and pea shoots.

5. **Make daily observations:** Check up on your plants once or twice every other day. You might need to carry out some tasks like:

    a. Watering to improve moisture.
    b. Checking for symptoms of mold formation.
    c. Ensuring adequate air circulation and light positioning.
    d. Acting speedily to revive conditions like weakness or forward inclination.
    e. Taking off the lid, especially if you grow them in an enclosed container.
    f. Moving the plants to another space for easier access to better light for photosynthesis. This could save you the risk of leggy and spindly growth.

6. **Soil composition**: For quick, healthy, and thick growth, it is necessary to be aware of the nutrients in your seed mix. Once the seeds have germinated and spring their first true leaves, their continued healthy development rests on the moisture, light, and growing medium available to them.

Microgreens don't require quite as much nutrition as seedlings as they don't need to grow into mature plants. Certain mixes for cultivating seeds have little to no nutrients or high sodium levels. Other growing media may tend to hold more moisture than required, thus blocking potential air pockets. Such mixes could lead to problems like damping and root rot.

While microgreens can grow and thrive in a plethora of growing media, they do vary in nutrient content and requirement over time. You can take charge of the flavor intensity, color vibrance, nutrient richness and content, and healthiness by creating your own seed growing mix. You can add trace elements and all the necessary minerals required for healthy growth. A good idea is to use liquid seaweed solutions daily or once every two days.

7. **Try repurposing seed raising mix**: While it is a bad idea to reuse the mix you used in growing your microgreens, it can come in handy when repurposed. After harvesting all your microgreens, there tends to be some leftover seeds and roots. The seeds could be as a result of not having enough room to grow and mature. If you continue to nurture the mix, you could get a second growth in due time. There's no point doing away with your seed mix now, is there?

After totally harvesting all your microgreens, the seed raising mix will be overrun with unharvested roots. Over time, it will break down and add to the organic matter content of the soil. However, without additional time and processing, trying to plant new seeds into the mix would be unwise, as there won't be room for sufficient growth and germination.

Also, you run the risk of the seed becoming contaminated by plant pathogens due to the composting process. To avoid this, try repurposing your seed raising mix by adding it to a worm farm or allowing it to compost totally. Afterward, you can use it again in your growing media for new seeds. This way, you've recycled nutrients and saved money so that you can plant more microgreens over time.

Is Microgreen Consumption Risky?

In a general sense, consuming microgreens is quite safe. However, it is noteworthy that these plants pose the risk of food poisoning. Since the probability of bacteria growth in microgreens is significantly less than in sprouts, they are a much safer alternative. Microgreens can be cultivated in environments that are less humid and warm than is necessary for sprouts, and only the stems and leaves are eaten as opposed to the seeds and roots. With that in mind, for people planning to cultivate microgreens on a small scale, getting the seeds from a reputable company is important. Also, it's important to ensure that the growing medium is devoid of contamination by harmful bacteria like *E. Coli* and *Salmonella*.

Common growing mediums for microgreens include vermiculite, perlite, and peat. Also, there are single-use growing mats specifically designed for the cultivation of microgreens. These are deemed to have high sanitary standards.

Introducing Microgreen into Your Food

This can be done in many different ways. One way is to incorporate them into a variety of dishes, such as salads, wraps, and sandwiches. Asides direct inclusion in food, they could also be juiced or blended into smoothies. For example, a common juiced form of microgreens is wheatgrass juice. Another alternative use is for garnishing dishes, such as omelets, pizzas, curries, and soups, among other warm foods.

In this light, microgreens are relatively safe. However, there are some cases in which they aren't. For instance, sprouts aren't consumed raw, due to the conditions in which they are grown (poor sunlight, ventilation, dampness, and soils). These conditions spur the growth and multiplication of fungi and bacteria, which may be harmful to health. Similarly, the soil preparation for microgreens cultivation requires lots of nutrients, which could lead to a mold growth problem.

On the other hand, microgreens do have a rather clean cultivation process, being grown in safer and cleaner conditions. However, this doesn't completely eliminate the risk of them containing harmful microbes when consumed raw. Thus, it is best to consume them after they've been rinsed off. Since the root isn't being consumed and is left out during harvesting, this also slashes the contamination potential down significantly.

But the absence of the root doesn't necessarily imply a total elimination of pathogens on microgreens. And what better way to combat microbes than good old fashion cooking, which fights off fungus, parasites, bacteria, and even spores? However, since cooking tends to reduce the nutrient integrity of microgreens, they are seldom ever cooked. The reason is that some of the enzymes and vitamins in microgreens are water-soluble. With that in mind, it's important to note the microgreens that could pose certain health risks, particularly when consumed too much.

These microgreens have a specific chemical content, which is mildly toxic to the human system. The body can handle such toxicity in small quantities, so those microgreens are entirely safe provided you follow certain instructions. Below are some of those microgreens:

1. **Quinoa**: This microgreen contains saponins, which are an anti-nutrient. However, these saponins can be easily removed during cultivation. To do this, try soaking the seeds in water, after which you run and rinse them several times to clear the soap-like suds. Quinoa seeds sold in packets tend to be pretreated to remove this quality, so you could purchase those instead.
2. **Alfalfa**: This microgreen is popular for its petite structure and is typically used raw in several soups and delicacies. However, it has a high germ content, hence there is a higher probability of infection outbreaks in its consumers. Additionally, this microgreen has a fair percentage of unhealthy compounds, including canavanine (an amino acid), and lectins and saponins, which are both anti-nutrients. While the body can handle these unhealthy compounds in small quantities, they tend to result in

bloating, inflammation, indigestion, diarrhea, and symptoms similar to lupus, caused by the canavanine content, when consumed in large amounts.
3. **Buckwheat**: This is a microgreen with a fast growth cycle. It contains a compound known as fagopyrin, which can cause symptoms like swelling, redness, and burning sensations on the skin when consumed in large amounts. It makes the skin highly sensitive to sunlight, and this symptom can persist for several days. These symptoms tend to vary across people. Many reportedly haven't experienced some of these symptoms, even when consumed in bulk several times a week. Some suggest that a different variety from India could be responsible, with consuming the common local variety having a much different outcome.

Chapter 3

Types of Microgreens

Microgreens are tasty, beautiful, and nutritious. But there's more to why they are as popular as they are today: variety. With microgreens, variety is indeed the spice of life. There is no shortage of choice with microgreens. So, let's check a few of them out.

Generally, there are six popular families of microgreens.

1. Radish, cauliflower, and arugula are classified under **Brassicaceae**.
2. In the **Asteraceae** family, we have veggies like endives and lettuces.
3. Cucumbers and melons are **Cucurbitaceaes**.
4. Carrots and celery are categorized as **Apiaceaes**.
5. The **Amaranthaceae** family consists of quinoa, spinach, and beets.
6. Garlic, leeks, and onions, belongs to the **Amaryllidaceae** family.

Knowing that, let's outline some microgreens and their unique characteristics.

Arugula

Called by many names (roquette, rocket, and colewort, among others), arugula is naturally filled with antioxidants, folic acid, vitamin C, and vitamin A. This means that consuming arugula is not just good for dealing with free radicals, but also quite effective with digestion. This microgreen also contains necessary minerals such as calcium, iron, potassium,

Arugula can be grown in soil or with hydroponics. This makes it a good plant for people who like the control hydroponics offers. It has a germination period of about two days and you can harvest the plant in little over a week. The harvest period is usually no more than 8 days.

Asparagus

Otherwise known as sparrow grass, asparagus is prone to delayed germination. This does not mean that you shouldn't cultivate them. But they must be pre-soaked for at least 5 hours to wake the asparagus seeds from their dormant state.

With pre-soaking, the germination time should be around 7 days. But, you will have to wait for a minimum of 20 days to harvest the microgreens. Asparagus contains vitamin A, vitamin C, iron, magnesium, and potassium.

Barley

Barley microgreens are quite nutritious. That is, if you can get past the feeling that you're just eating grass. This grass taste is what turns many people away from consuming barley microgreens.

But, guess who doesn't mind eating grass and find barley microgreens really delicious. Livestock, dogs, and cats. They just absolutely love to munch on these greens, Rabbits can't seem to get enough of them as well. So, many times when people purchase these microgreens, they do so for their animals.

Just in case you can overlook that grassy and earthy taste, then you'd be doing your body a world of good by eating these greens.

Barley can be germinated in just 2 days, sometimes less. Their harvest time is often in little over a week. These microgreens are good for those who have diabetes and can help prevent some cancers and heart diseases. They are rich in dietary fiber, beta-carotene, vitamin E, and protein.

Basil

There are different kinds of basil microgreens and they all come with their own unique, interesting taste. Lemon Basil, Cinnamon Basil, Holy Basil, and Red Rubin Basil are just a few of them. Whether you want zesty, spicy, or sweet, basil has these varieties and more.

One downside to growing basil could be the fact that it takes a while to germinate and to become ready for harvest when planted in a cold region or climate. In the winter, harvest time can be up to two weeks. This might not seem like a long time, but two weeks isn't exactly a quick harvest in the context of microgreens. Basil microgreens can germinate in between 2-3 days.

Basil seeds are mucilaginous. This means that the seeds protect themselves from unfavorable environmental conditions by forming a gel-like capsule when they get wet. It also means that they are terribly affected by clumping. They should be spread evenly and inches apart from each other.

You can get vitamin A, C, and K, and high polyphenols from consuming basil microgreens.

Beets

This microgreen takes the most time to germinate - as much as 21 days. This means that, as a planter, you might have to wait for more than a month before harvesting your microgreen beets. When they are ready to be harvested, the beets will have a bright red stem and light green flowers. They have a taste that is similar to, but sweeter than, beetroot.

They're very easy to plant so they're great for beginners, but keep in mind that they need to be pre-soaked for about 10 hours or they won't germinate quickly enough. Most of the time, beets will germinate in 7-14 days if they are pre-soaked, and they can be harvested in 8-12 days. It is possible to grow beet microgreens in a hydroponic system but growing them in soil is generally the best method.

The taste of beets is similar to sweet chards. Although you could, of course, disagree with that. Beets are packed with potassium, calcium, protein, magnesium, zinc, and iron. They also contain vitamins A, B, C, E, and K, lutein, and beta-carotene.

Broccoli

These microgreens contain a substance called sulforaphane. It is beneficial to your health but does cause the broccoli to taste a little bitter. But not everyone reports that the broccoli microgreen is bitter. When the sulforaphane compound is not present, some say it has a mild broccoli taste.

With just a two-day germination time and a one week harvest time, it can be said that broccoli microgreens are quick to cultivate. They also contain vitamins A, C, and K. But if that isn't enough incentive to consume broccoli, they are also good preventative measures against lung and colon cancers. They also improve digestion and bone health.

Buckwheat

Hydroponics can be used to grow buckwheat. Although, it is not advised. This is because the process of growing this plant without soil is not particularly easy. Buckwheat should be kept in a humidity dome before they can safely be exposed to light. It's usually much better to just grow them traditionally. Buckwheat needs about 4 days to germinate and 7-14 days to fully mature. As a gardener, make sure to water your buckwheat once a day. Make sure it's also at the same time of the day. You want the soil to be neither dry nor soggy.

Buckwheat contains fiber, vitamin C, vitamin B, vitamin K, and folic acid.

Cabbage

Arguably, the most popular kind of cabbages are the green and red kinds. People often choose the red cabbage because it is considered the sweetest and has more vitamin C. The green cabbage contains more folate, which is a type of vitamin B that promotes the production of red and white blood cells and is needed during adolescence, pregnancy, and infancy.

Germination time for cabbage is 2-3 days, but you might have to wait 2 weeks for harvest. It's quite soft when chewed and can be really colorful on a dish - with violet stems and green tops. Cabbage provides iron, vitamin C, beta-carotene, vitamin K, and vitamin E.

Carrot

They take some time to be ready for harvest - about two weeks - but the result is a rewardingly nutritious microgreen. Using the soil method to plant carrot microgreens is considered the best way since it leads to a faster germination time.

Carrot microgreens don't have a lot to offer in terms of taste. But with nutrients like folate, calcium, sodium, and vitamin A, C, and K, they really aren't a bad addition to any meal.

Cauliflower

This crispy and flavorful vegetable is seen as one of the more easily grown microgreens. Cauliflower stems are a very light pink and purple, while the tops are a deep green. You can grow them successfully in the soil or with hydroponics. The germination time for cauliflower is between 2 to 3 days, and they can be harvested in about 2 weeks after planting.

You can get beta-carotene, iron, vitamin C, and vitamin E from eating cauliflower.

Celosia

Usually, the leaves of microgreens are green, while their stem has a different color. The case is different for celosia. Their stems are green, and they have light red leaves. They really are a pleasant sight to behold and their mild taste just completes their beauty. They have a three-day maximum germination time and can be harvested in 12 days.

As for nutritional benefits, celosia microgreens contain an abundance of calcium, phosphorus, iron, and water.

Chervil

If you love parsley, licorice, or anise, then you will enjoy chervil. While this microgreen is definitely unique, it does manage to blend these three flavors perfectly. It does this so well, in fact, that some refer to it as French parsley. They can be harvested as early as 12 days after planting, but most gardeners would wait till at least the 16th day in order to get that beautiful mix of tastes.

Germination time for chervil microgreens is in no more than 4 days, and they provide vitamins A, B, C, and D. You can also get iron, potassium, calcium, and protein from eating chervil.

Corn

The microgreen shoots of corn are usually much sweeter than mature corn. Although this depends on some factors. One is that you need to harvest the microgreens on or before the sixth day of planting. If you wait for longer, the leaves will show up, and you don't want to eat those. They contain way too much fiber and aren't exactly pleasant to eat.

The other thing you should do is make sure light does not get to the shoots. This is one reason why some gardeners might prefer hydroponics. You can grow the corn microgreens indoors and in the dark. Sunlight on the shoots causes the plant to become too fibrous and develop its leaves.

Corn microgreens can be germinated in three days max. The harvest time is between 12 and 16 days. This microgreen contains calcium, magnesium, and vitamin A, B, C, and E.

Endive

We've mentioned microgreens that are enjoyed for their tastiness. Some, like radishes, are spicy. Others are slightly sweet, like cauliflower. Endives, on the other hand, are a sharp contrast. They are mildly bitter, and it is for this particular reason that people like to cultivate them. If you are into a variety of tastes in your sandwiches, microgreen salads, and other meals, then you will enjoy endives.

On the tenth day after planting, you can usually harvest the microgreens. Depending on certain environmental factors, you might have to wait 15 days to harvest them. Typically, endives enter their adult stages on the 16th day. The germination time for endives is 3 days. Soil is the best way to grow endive baby greens. For endive microgreens, hydroponics wins.

Endives contain beta-carotene, vitamin K, folate, pantothenic acid, vitamin A, manganese, calcium, zinc, and many other vital nutrients.

Lettuce

The germination time for lettuces can take up to 4 days. They thrive under moderate heat, humidity, and constant water. This means that hydroponics is great for lettuces. The stems of lettuce are often light green. Sometimes, they are a pale white color.

The nutrients contained in your lettuce include fiber, vitamin B, vitamin K, vitamin C, and folic acid.

Mustard

Like corn, your mustard needs to do some growing in the dark. But there's a difference. The mustard seeds should spend just two days in darkness. Afterward, you can expose them to sunlight or your grow light. Under the right conditions, mustard seeds grow pretty fast. They can reach maturity in only 12 days, and this similarity is shared by most microgreens in the Brassicaceae family.

Mustard seeds are rich in vitamins A, C, E, and K, fiber, and antioxidants.

Radish

People often go for radishes because of how colorful they can be. With their red stems and vibrantly green leaves, it's little wonder that quite a number of people are taken by this microgreen. For others, their choice of radishes has little to do with its colors. They just love the spiciness. Radishes aren't so hot that they can't be enjoyed. But they still pack a kick that spice lovers keep coming back for.

Radishes take as little as a day or two to germinate. For the harvest, you need only wait 6-12 days. They can be grown in soil or hydroponically. They are deliciously crunchy and packed with vitamins A, B, C, E, and K. Your radish also contains niacin, calcium, zinc, iron, and phosphorus.

Differences Between Microgreens and Baby Greens

As stated earlier, microgreens share some similarities with baby greens. Both are harvested before they can attain maturity and contain more nutrients than fully grown veggies. For these reasons, people often confuse both greens to mean the same things. Not quite.

After seeds are planted, the next stage is sprouting. It is unlikely that you have seen this stage as it typically happens beneath the soil.

Although, because of how nutrient-rich sprouts are, some folks grow them at home for consumption.

Fast forward a few days (or weeks) and you have your microgreens. At this point, the plant has now developed stems, roots, and cotyledons - the first leaves. Even though these cotyledons are not mature leaves, they can still perform the function of photosynthesis.

If you allow the microgreens to grow some more, you will have the baby greens. These plants are not fully matured, but they have outgrown cotyledons for true leaves. Usually, plants are more nutritious the less mature they are. This means that sprouts are richer than microgreens. And microgreens have more nutrients than baby greens.

Popular Microgreens and Their Nutritional Value

The serving size for these microgreens is 100 g, and the nutritional value is for raw greens.

Arugula

Calories: 25 Total Fat: 0.7 g Sodium: 27 mg Total Carbs: 3.7 g Protein: 2.6 g Potassium: 369 mg Cholesterol: 0 mg

Beets

Calories: 43 Total Fat: 0.2 g Sodium: 78 mg Total Carbs: 9.6 g Protein: 1.6 g Potassium: 325 mg Iron: 0.80 mg

Buckwheat

Calories: 343 Total Fat: 3.4 g Sodium: 1 mg Total Carbs: 72 g Protein: 13 g Potassium: 460 mg Iron: 2.20 mg

Cabbage

Calories: 25 Total Fat: 0.1 g Sodium: 18 mg Total Carbs: 6 g Protein: 1.3 g Potassium: 170 mg Iron: 0.47 mg

Cauliflower

Calories: 25 Total Fat: 0.3 g Sodium: 30 mg Total Carbs: 5 g Protein: 1.9 g Potassium: 299 mg Cholesterol: 0 mg

Corn

Calories: 86 Total Fat: 1.2 g Sodium: 15 mg Total Carbs: 19 g Protein: 3.2 g Potassium: 270 mg Iron: 0.52 mg

Endives

Calories: 17 Total Fat: 0.2 g Sodium: 22 mg Total Carbs: 3.4 g Protein: 1.3 g Potassium: 314 mg Iron: 0.83 mg

Lettuce

Calories: 15 Total Fat: 0.2 g Sodium: 28 mg Total Carbs: 2.9 g Protein: 1.4 g Potassium: 194 mg Cholesterol: 0 mg

Mustard

Calories: 27 Total Fat: 0.4 g Sodium: 20 mg Total Carbs: 4.7 g Protein: 2.9 g Potassium: 384 mg Iron: 1.64 mg

Radish

Calories: 16 Total Fat: 0.1 g Sodium: 39 mg Total Carbs: 3.4 g Protein: 0.7 g Potassium: 233 mg Cholesterol: 0 mg

Chapter 4

Microgreen Troubleshooting Tips

As excited as you might be to begin cultivating your own microgreens, you must understand that the process isn't always entirely smooth. Even with the simplest of methods, things could still go wrong. Sometimes, awfully so. And the proper thing to do is prepare yourself for such eventualities.

Now you're probably wondering which eventualities, right? Here they are.

Mold

For most beginner growers, there will be no escaping this problem. Those who use hydroponics are more prone to this issue. A few things could give rise to mold or mildew as you grow your microgreens. It could be that your plant's environment is too soggy. While greens need sufficient amounts of moisture to grow well, it's also important that there isn't too much water.

High levels of humidity, poor ventilation, and inadequate supply of direct light are also contributing factors to the growth of mold and mildew.

In some cases, the problem really isn't mold or anything similar. Sometimes, those who aren't experienced in gardening might confuse the structure of root hairs for mildew.

To differentiate the two (root hair and mildew), just keep these tips in mind.

1. Root hair is only found on the roots, and mildew can be found even between the microgreens.
2. Root hair appears fuzzy, while mildew seems more like a spider's web.
3. If you rinse the roots, the root hairs will disappear for hours. Mildew will remain visible even after rinsing.
4. Mildew has a slimy feel, while root hairs do n0t.
5. Root hair has no smell to it, but mildew is quite musty.

Troubleshooting Mold

1. Sometimes, the environment is perfect and it is the seedlings themselves that demand your attention. Seeds are not healthy by default and shouldn't be planted without proper sanitization. This is where pre-soaking comes into play. The time needed for pre-soaking is not the same for every seed, and the temperature of the water also differs. Generally, you can let seeds sit in a bowl of water containing one teaspoon of hydrogen peroxide for about 3 hours.

   This not only reduces the chances of mold growth but the germination time as well. You can expect a quicker harvest than if you hadn't pre-soaked the seeds.

2. Gardeners often go a step further and choose hybrid seeds that are able to resist mold growth. Your chances of getting a good buy, of course, depends on the company you're purchasing from. As such, you want to only buy seeds from trusted brands. The seeds are to be of the highest quality.

3. If there are too many people in a room with limited air supply, a single toilet, as much food as they need, and no way to get out - you can tell how that situation would go, first a messy problem, then tragic. The same goes for crops that are suffering from overseeding. As they sprout, become seedlings, and then

microgreens, it will become increasingly difficult to get air to reach the individual plants.

And this is just right for mold formation. With the area in mind, it is important to keep a few inches between the seeds. The less dense your seedlings are, the less likely you'll have to deal with mold.

4. Since the most common cause of mold formation is an overly wet environment, you have to find a solution for this. The design for most hydroponic systems already comes with a good way to handle this problem: drainage. It has to allow for proper soil aeration and prevent erosion.

Fallen Greens

One of the hardest things to watch is a microgreen leaning over and slowly, but certainly, wilting. Without question, it hurts to watch something you've put quite a bit of effort into turn brown and lifeless.

There are a number of reasons for microgreens to keel over in this way. Too little water supply, poor environmental factors (temperature, light, humidity, nutrients, pH, etc.), and overseeding are just a few of them.

But there are ways to prevent this from happening. And even if the microgreens lie seemingly lifeless, there are ways to revive them.

Troubleshooting Fallen Greens

1. You will find that water - whether in excess or otherwise - is the cause of many of the problems that affect microgreens. And when it comes to plants falling over, water is often the problem and solution.

   Try adding some water to your microgreens, and they will most likely bounce back. Remember that microgreens need water in varying amounts. Radishes, for instance, need a lot of water to grow healthy, while quinoa needs far less.

So, to fix the problem, you shouldn't just water the microgreens. You need to learn how much that particular green needs and provide it.

2. Upon planting your seeds, the expectation is that they will grow as tall as they need to. But there is such a thing as too tall. When this happens, the stem becomes too thin and weak. Eventually, the plants succumb to gravity and fall.

This (microgreens getting too tall) is usually the result of leaving the plants in the dark for longer than necessary. They will continue growing upward and eventually the stems will no longer be thick enough to support them. The longer the microgreens stay in darkness, the thinner they will be.

The simple solution here is to expose the plants to sunlight when it's due.

Yellow Microgreens

If you are new to planting microgreens, this could seem like a serious problem and might even cause some panic. While it's unusual, it doesn't mean the end of your crops. This issue is caused by not taking off the blackout dome soon enough. Since they haven't been exposed to sunlight, the seedlings will turn yellow.

Troubleshooting Yellow Microgreens

1. All you need to do is remove the blackout dome. For most greens, it's even better if you take it off early. Afterward, make sure the plants get adequate sunlight.

Clumped Greens

This happens for the same reason as the mold problem: planting too many seeds in the same area. Gardeners, even experienced ones, plant large numbers of seeds because they want a higher yield. Often, this ends up being counterproductive.

There are always a finite number of resources that different plants can struggle for. With the issue of clumps, the resource is the area of land you are cultivating. Since there isn't enough space between each seed, the microgreens will push against each other as they grow. Some plants may be lifted out of the soil with their roots exposed.

Troubleshooting Clumped Greens
1. The first and most obvious solution is to allow for more space between each seed. This also means decreasing the number of seeds you plant in a single area. You have a better chance of getting higher yields if you plant fewer seeds.
2. The second tip is to make sure that your seeds are spread evenly on the tray. This can be a little difficult at first, but it will eliminate the problem of clumps.

Slow Germination Time

As we've learned from chapter three, microgreens typically grow really fast. Most, taking no more than 4 days. But this isn't always the case. You might notice if you try to cultivate a microgreen, that it takes longer than it should to germinate. If you are certain that the seed has gone past its normal germination time, there are a few things you can do.

Troubleshooting Slow Germination Time
1. The first thing you should make sure of is that the seeds are of the best quality. Before you plant them, perform a germination test by covering the seeds with a wet paper towel.

2. You could also try to enhance the germination of your plants by placing a heavy object on them. The item should be weighted, but not so heavy that it completely crushes them.
3. Finally, there is pre-soaking. This is a good way to "wake" the seeds up. Different seeds require varying pre-soak times. Some need just 4 hours, while others might require up to 12 hours of pre-soaking.

Chapter 5

How to Grow Microgreens at Home

So, you've decided to cultivate microgreens. That's great. You should understand that nothing is ever entirely an easy process. But the process of growing microgreens is not just fun, it is also quite rewarding. Let's get right to it.

When it comes to microgreens, there are a host of plants to grow. From buckwheat to beets and lettuces. Just take your pick.

Some of the things you will need to start growing these vegetables are;

1. Grow light. Alternatively, you can find a window in the south-side of your chosen room that also has good access to sunlight.
2. A shallow container where you will add you grow media and seeds.
3. A warming mat. This isn't a compulsory tool, but it does help to hasten germination.
4. Your preferred microgreen seeds.
5. Growing media and organic soil.

Cultivating Your Microgreens

1. The first thing you want to do is find that part of the room where adequate sunlight can get to your plants. If you would rather use a grow light, that's fine. They aren't expensive either. The grow lights allow for more mobility and flexibility. You can plant your microgreens anywhere you feel is more comfortable and even at times of the year when there isn't much sunlight.

2. It's time to do some clearing. If you will be planting outdoors, clear a small area of land. For indoor planting, add the organic soil to the bottom of your tray. It should rise only an inch up from the bottom of the tray. Even the soil out.
3. Now, you can spread the seeds on the soil. Make sure the seeds are even. Pre-soak the seeds the night before to speed up the time it will take the seeds to sprout.
4. Again, add soil to your tray. This soil is to cover the seeds, and this should also be even. Spray clean water on the soil. Contaminated water can lead to serious problems later on, so make sure the water has been filtered.
5. Next, you can keep the container in the part of the room that receives the most sunlight. Alternatively, place it under your grow light.
6. For a few days afterward, continue spraying the clean, filtered water onto the soil. Sogginess is a problem, but so is dryness.
7. In about 4 days, the seeds should have germinated and microgreens should appear before 4 weeks. Harvest them.
8. You can cut off the roots of the microgreens and replant them. You could also replace everything in the container. The choice is entirely yours.

Benefits of Growing Microgreens

1. Depending on the variety of plants you are cultivating, microgreens grow quite fast. Whether you want to sell them or are just growing them for personal consumption, you can harvest your microgreens in 3 weeks or less.
2. You want a quick yield. You want a high yield. But, something you probably don't know you want yet is a high yield/space ratio. Even though you should not attempt to grow too many seeds in a small area, you *can* grow an impressive amount in a small space.

3. You will need to spend a relatively small amount of time, effort, and money to cultivate any microgreen of your choice. In only a short while, you can cultivate your "fast food". The amount of money, time, or effort you will have to spend will depend mostly on the system of cultivation you use. For example, soil-less or hydroponic methods are often more expensive to set up.
4. As a result of how little space is needed to cultivate microgreens, they are a good fit for people who don't have enough room to do any planting. If you are also very busy, then you want to cultivate plants that won't require too much maintenance and grow quickly: microgreens.
5. There are only a few things needed to cultivate microgreens. If you have your growing medium, a shallow container (tray) for planting, the seeds, good lighting, and water, then you're good to go. Depending on the technique of cultivation you choose, you might need more or fewer things. But, generally, microgreens don't need much. This means you'll save money by planting microgreens.
6. Microgreens have been known to thrive regardless of climate. The season doesn't matter as much as you think it would. Hot or cold; rainy or arid; microgreens have a great chance at survival. This is not to mean that you can abandon the plants to fend entirely for themselves. But if you play your part by pre-soaking seeds, providing water, managing the environment, etc., then you have a high probability of getting a good yield regardless of the time of year you're planting.
7. And we can't complete this list without considering the fact that microgreens are typically nutrient-dense foods. They are packed with so many nutrients and are so healthy that there is another list in this book outlining the health benefits of microgreens. Check the next chapter.

Microgreens are a tasty, aesthetically satisfying, nutritious, and incredibly palatable food choice.

Chapter 6

Health Benefits of Eating Microgreens

Everyone from your doctor to your grandma knows that eating veggies is linked to a reduced susceptibility to developing certain diseases. And since microgreens are, well, greens, you know that they are one of the healthiest things to consume. These benefits stem from the high volume of plant compounds, minerals, and vitamins they contain. Below are some benefits of eating microgreens.

1. **It reduces the risk of heart problems**: Microgreens have a high polyphenol content, a category of antioxidants related to decreasing the risk of developing heart problems. Studies of this quality in animals revealed that microgreens may, in fact, reduce poor LDL cholesterol levels and decrease triglycerides in the body. A study carried out on rats fed a diet with high fat content that was supplemented with red cabbage microgreens showed a decline in weight gain by up to 17%. Furthermore, triglycerides were down by 23%, while bad LDL cholesterol decreased by 34% (Huang, 2016).
2. **It lowers the chance of chronic ailments:** Vegetables have been shown to have great health benefits, as a result of their nutrient value and polyphenol levels. Thus, vegetable consumption has been linked to the reduction of specific types of chronic ailments. Vegetable intake decreases the risk of inflammation, as well as lowering the risk of obesity. Since microgreens have a

very similar nutritional and polyphenol content, more even in comparison to mature plants, they likely also have many benefits in tackling these ailments.

3. **It helps prevent Alzheimer's disease:** Due to their high antioxidant content and richness in polyphenols, microgreens could prove handy in decreasing susceptibility to Alzheimer's disease.
4. **It prevents diabetes**: Since stress can inhibit proper sugar absorption on a cellular level, antioxidants can be helpful in combating this stress. Laboratory studies on fenugreek microgreens showed an improvement in the ability of cells to absorb sugar by as much as 25 to 44 percent. Microgreens are typically found to have an effect on type 2 diabetes.
5. **Microgreens are convenient and easy to use:** For people who haven't really turned to regular consumption of vegetables and fruits, microgreens can come in handy in helping get started. Lots of people enjoy growing microgreens as they are easier, faster, and more convenient to cultivate. As a matter of fact, one need not have a full-scale garden or a backyard to cultivate or raise microgreens. Provided one has a bit of water, the seeds, soil, and a source of light (window), that is enough to start a mini garden of microgreens. Most importantly, microgreens come in handy for new and impatient gardeners.

The wait time for cultivating microgreens is minimal as these plants can be grown, harvested, and ready for use within 7 to 14 days past germination.

6. **It can help fight certain cancers:** The antioxidant content in vegetables and fruits, particularly those with equally high polyphenol content, can help decrease one's susceptibility to certain types of cancer. Although not all forms of cancer are easily combated, those typically affected by vegetables include

cancers of the digestive tract and prostate cancer. Microgreens with high levels of polyphenol may have similar qualities.

Chapter 7

Some Microgreen FAQs

1. What are microgreens?

They are younger plants, usually vegetables, that are harvested at about 1-3 weeks after planting. This is just after they produce their cotyledons or first leaves. However, not every microgreen can be eaten at the same stage, as some must be allowed to mature further and others need to be harvested early. Microgreens are becoming more popular because they provide dishes with a wide range of flavor, look, texture, and nutritional benefits.

2. Are there risks in eating microgreens?

Microgreens are often consumed raw, and this means that it is necessary to care for them diligently when they are still growing. First, since they may be grown in humid conditions and in close proximity to each other, water can be trapped leading to decay and mildew growth. Be sure to space your seeds far enough apart and ensure adequate ventilation to prevent this. Also, ensure that your plants are not exposed to infectious organisms like bacteria or fungi from other plants. Finally, ensure you buy your seeds from a reputable source such as a supermarket chain or well-known farm that performs regular and strict food safety checks.

Also, consider the water source. Do not use water that may be contaminated, like spring water or rain water that has not been treated. Planting microgreens outdoors may expose them to worms and insects. Also, check properly to ensure the microgreens you're buying are not moldy or rotten and that it has not been eaten by insects.

3. How can microgreens be grown at home?

With hydroponics, you can grow microgreens without the need for fertilizer and soil. The basics are just water, a nutrient mix, and light and it can be done commercially. You can easily grow microgreens in your home. Be careful while handling them because they are fragile young plants. Don't forget to make sure the seeds have enough room for growth and germination.

They appear small but that doesn't take away their need for adequate air circulation. The microgreens will decay if their surroundings are too stuffy or humid. Don't place them directly under the sunlight. A suitable temperature range for them is 77-90°F (25 - 32°C).

4. What is the best way to care for microgreens?

You can care for microgreens if you grow them in coconut coir water or thin mat water. A low maintenance method would be by placing the greens on a cookie tray. Cover with a lid and pour in a cup of water every day. Another option is to let them remain in their containers and open the lid so that condensation will not occur. If condensation occurs, the greens wither and die. If you will be away for some time, place them in a cool room with a temperature of less than 75°F (24°C) and good ventilation or in the fridge. They will be viable for 7-10 days without regular care with this method.

5. Which microgreens are the easiest to grow?

The brassica family is known for being easy to grow. Members of this family include cauliflower, broccoli, cabbages, etc. Another easy microgreen is anything in the mustard family. Chia is known as one of the easiest microgreens. Growers who use a hydroponic microgreens kit are provided with the easiest seeds, this is especially helpful if they are just starting. But for those planting in soil, the easiest microgreens are buckwheat and sunflower.

6. Which microgreens are most difficult to grow?

Some of the more difficult microgreens include beets, amaranth, and arugula. Some also find it tough to grow chard and chives. However, stepping up to the challenge of growing these tough microgreens is the reason why it's an interesting pastime.

7. Can microgreens grow back after cutting? (How is it done?)

No. Regrowth is not common.

However, the microgreen still has a good survival rate if it has a minimum of one healthy leaf remaining. This is due to the fact that photosynthesis will be ongoing in the presence of light. But there will be a slower growth rate and this will eventually cause stunted growth.

Also, microgreens that are obtained from second harvests do not taste exactly the same as those from the first harvest

But there are some with better chances of regrowth like snow peas, speckled peas, field peas, green peas, and fava beans. Although the rate of regrowth for most other microgreens can be described as negligible. There is also a chance that what you see as regrown microgreens may just be late sprouted seeds.

Well, this just goes to show that trying for a second harvest may not be a good idea. Rather than dwelling on that, you can turn the remains from your harvest into compost.

8. Which seeds should be pre-soaked?

You should pre-soak sunflower, pea, and buckwheat seeds for 6 to 8 hours in cold water before planting them. Beet seeds should be pre-soaked, also in cold water, for a duration of one to two hours. In addition, broccoli, kale, chard, and radish seeds would benefit from pre-soaking. Note that seeds which become coated with a gel-like substance after contacting moisture may be difficult to spread after pre-soaking, so many choose not to soak them. These include basil, mustard, flax, and chia.

9. Why is it necessary to cover the microgreens so that they're in the dark for some time?

One important requirement for growing a microgreen into a long and superfine seedling is to cover it in the dark.

When it gets dark, the microgreens seek a light source by stretching out. The result is a longer, thinner and very tender microgreen. This may look good but there is only a small amount of starch in the endosperm, and eventually, the microgreens will use up all the energy and fall over. This is the reason for pegging the blackout phase at about 1-3 days after germination for a period of 3-5 days.

Photosynthesis will start as soon as you expose them to light, and the microgreens will become sturdy and thicker. Don't forget, however, that some microgreens are naturally short and will not increase much in height.

10. When is the right time to let microgreens receive light?

As stated above, most microgreens should be exposed to light only after blocking the light out for 3-5 days. The microgreens will start to look yellowish and pale. However, this duration is not suitable for all microgreens. You have to consider some factors. For instance, there are some microgreens that grow slowly like oregano or thyme, and they require stretching for longer periods in the dark. The ideal duration for this group is 5-8 days. But the fast growers like kale and broccoli can do just fine with 2-3 days of darkness.

Another thing to consider is the environment, cultivars, and seed quality.

You need to be very alert because the microgreens do not hesitate to turn green soon after they are exposed to light. The shoot thickens according to the increase in the production of glucose. When they are at this stage, you need to increase the water supply and prevent mold infestation by creating an effective air ventilation system.

11. When should microgreens be watered?

Large clusters of microgreens are often grown in a small area, and one factor that determines their survival is the water capacity. In fact, it is a lack of water that often makes the microgreens fall over. The normal process is to maintain the moisture by watering the microgreens' tray twice daily.

Consider the soil mixture and the local weather pattern (temperature and humidity) before you water.

Basically, good soil is one that allows water to drain out quickly so the environment is not soggy but also leaves the microgreen with enough water.

You can lighten your soil by adding 20% perlite. That way, the root has access to more air which boosts its water retention capacity.

Do an inspection on the upper and lower soil to check that it is not soggy but wet enough. The bottom watering option is better for small and feathery microgreens. When you use it, simply top up water to it every other day. Don't forget to raise the tray up before you check.

There are microgreens that naturally require more water, like the dun pea and the sunflower, and there are those that don't like the broccoli and cress. But generally, microgreens need more water as they grow bigger.

12. At what point do I use soil vs. hydroponics?

Microgreens can always be grown in soil. It may be difficult to cultivate some crops using hydroponics like pea, sunflower, beet, buckwheat, cilantro, etc. For these, you will likely have more success with a soil-based growing method, kits for this are available commercially. For other microgreens, you can definitely try a hydroponic system if you prefer.

13. Are growing lights very important?

Growing lights can be useful when it comes to exposing your microgreens to light at the right time and in the right amount. However, they are not required as you can expose microgreens to fluorescent light, direct sunlight, or incandescent light instead. Grow lights, especially LED grow lights, are preferable because they are lightweight, do not use much energy, and emit very little heat. Not only that, but they also provide the plants with the blue and red parts of the spectrum that they need. Further, the grow light setup can be adjusted and timed exactly as the microgreens require.

14. What makes LED grow lights the wise choice for microgreens?

LED lights are superior because they don't emit heat and use less electricity when compared with normal grow lights. Other grow lights release white light which doesn't have the optimal spectrum for growing plants, examples of this type of light include fluorescent light and T-5 bulbs. Plants absorb the blue and red ends of the light spectrum in order to perform photosynthesis, and LED grow lights are created to provide plants with the exact light spectrum they need. LEDs are even better than sunlight in terms of making microgreens greener and healthier.

15. Why are some parts of my crops rotten?

There are a lot of things that can cause rot. The major reason is that water is very alkaline. To adjust your water to a suitable pH, use a pH balancing kit. Another reason could be that the seeds are being overwatered or they were planted too thickly.

16. Why are my crops wilting?

Crops wilt when they are not watered enough or they are exposed to excess heat.

17. Do I need to stabilize the pH of my water?

Balancing the pH of the water used in growing is highly important. Although most growers don't believe that pH matters, it does.

18. Why are my crops pale?

The crops are pale because they may not be absorbing enough light. Grow them outdoors or place them by a window to access sunlight. They may tilt towards the light so rotate frequently. Another better option is to use LED grow lights.

19. Why are there burned or dry sections on the leaves of my crops?

The reason for this is because the plants are either getting excess light or the light is coming too early.

20. What action should I take if I perceive a musty odor?

If you're using a hydroponic system, the odor usually occurs if the grow pad has been used for longer than 10 days. There is usually no odor before 10 days. However, you shouldn't see this as a problem, especially as the normal harvest time for most crops is 10 days. However, if you're using a soil-based system, the musty smell may be originating from excess moisture trapped in between microgreen stems. In this case, it is important to remove the moisture or the problem may escalate to rot or mold.

21. Why are my crops growing slowly?

The crops may be growing slowly because they are too cold. This could be especially prevalent if your trays are placed on granite countertops or tile. If you have to put them on countertops, use a towel as an insulator. If this doesn't solve your issue, consider obtaining a heating pad and placing it under your tray. If you're growing your microgreens outside, consider investing in a greenhouse.

22. What can I do to preserve my remaining microgreens if I need to go on a trip and would not be able to care for it?

Find an airtight container and line the bottom with a paper towel. Cut your leftover microgreens and put them into the container. Put another layer of paper towel on it. Place the container if cut microgreens in the refrigerator or carry them along with you. If you are carrying them along, use a cooler and ice pack to preserve it.

23. Are all microgreen growing mats or pads compostable?

Whether a growing mat or pad can be composted depends on whether it is biodegradable. For example, the hydroponic system Sure-to-Grow pads are not made from natural fiber so they cannot be composted, although some claim that they outperform other options. If you're interested in sustainable hydroponic growing, consider choosing an alternate mat such as a Micro Mat grow pad, which is made from wood fibers and can be composted. In the case of soil-based systems, you can compost the spent soil mat that the root structure of your crop holds together.

24. How can I differentiate between sprouts, microgreens, and baby salad greens?

They are different because they are various growth stages of a plant.

The sprouts represent the beginning of seed development and do not need a growing medium (soil). Instead, when they sprout, they are raised in a sprouting bag, jar or tray and then rinsed. They become edible immediately after the seeds germinate and are quite crunchy.

Microgreens are cultivated in a growing medium or soil. They mark the second stage of a plant's development. They become rooted and produce their first leaves (cotyledons), and at this point, they can be harvested before they begin to produce their true leaves. When plants are in the microgreens stage, they are tastier and have been able to soak in micronutrients and trace elements from the growth medium (soil).

Baby salad greens are attained by allowing the plant to grow for 1-2 weeks after the microgreen stage. At this stage, the true leaves have developed and the greens are harvested as young plants. The taste is a little closer to what it will be when they are adult plants.

25. *How nutritious are microgreens?*

Even though microgreens are harvested at a much earlier stage of growth than vegetables, their nutritional content is high. Research reports from the United States Department of Agriculture and other scientific journals state that microgreens have more nutritional value than adult vegetables. For instance, a regular gram of broccoli has two to three times less nutritional content than broccoli microgreens. Microgreens are known for their antioxidant properties.

26. *Do microgreens taste different than their vegetable counterparts?*

Because microgreens are eaten at a young stage, they have a more delicate and, arguably, enhanced taste when compared to adult vegetables. This delicate taste is why they are typically eaten raw and make great additions to salads or side dishes. However, their taste is determined by the species of vegetable and the farming method used. Thus, they will taste similar to their mature vegetable counterparts.

27. *What varieties of microgreens are most common?*

In theory, every vegetable has a microgreen which is the younger stage of its growth. But some microgreen species are more prominent because of their growth conditions, appearance, and taste. Some of the most famous ones include celery, lettuce, red cabbage, basil, kale, and spinach. Some less popular microgreens are buckwheat, radish, and mustard greens.

28. How long is the shelf life of microgreens?

The best time to eat microgreens is when they're fresh. This means buying them only when you're ready to eat them. If you can't get your microgreens the same day you want to eat them, then they can remain fresh if you keep them in the fridge, but first, wrap them in a damp paper towel. The handling conditions of the microgreens you're using differs according to the kind of plant the adult vegetable is. Don't use them in your dish until you have all the necessary information from the producer.

29. What is the best way to prepare microgreens?

Microgreens are delicate. As such, they are better used when served fresh. A lot of chefs use them as toppings for a fresh garden salad or to brighten up the color of another prepared dish or add zest to it. Only under very rare circumstances are they cooked. If the dish you have to prepare needs the microgreens to be heated, then don't forget that bad preparation can cause the microgreens to wilt quickly or burn. The best method of cooking is to saute it.

Sauteeing involves exposing the microgreens to very high heat for only a little time. It is simple to carry out. Just heat a little quantity of oil or butter in a pan. Don't use too much oil so that the microgreens do not drown inside. When the pan is hot enough, put in the microgreens and allow them to cook for just enough time to scorch the outside. This process traps the flavor and moisture in and keeps it from being soggy.

30. What types of meals can I add microgreens to?

Raw preparation is the best for microgreens. You can add them to your Burgers, Sandwiches, Salads, Tostadas, Tacos, Smoothies, Hotdogs, Wraps. Better still, just get different varieties and make a microgreen salad. You can eat your microgreens with everything.

31. How many microgreens should I eat?

Like all foods, you can eat as many as is healthy. Since microgreens are usually low in calories, you can eat quite a lot indeed.

32. Can pregnant women consume microgreens?

Generally, microgreens are safe for pregnant women. These women, however, are advised to not consume raw sprouts. This is because bacteria such as *E. coli* and *Salmonella* can easily get into the seeds and can result in premature birth or miscarriage. If the sprouts are well cooked (stir fried, for example), then it's alright for pregnant women to eat them. Sprouts differ from many microgreens in that their roots can be eaten.

33. What makes microgreens so expensive?

A large amount of labor is required to grow microgreens and this is why they are much more expensive than the adult leafy greens.

34. If I purchase microgreens, how can I wash them?

Microgreens are often delivered raw and unwashed to keep them fresh. Since they're raw, they should be washed. Simply rinse them under running water and pat them dry with a clean cloth or paper towel. Alternately, you can dry them in a salad spinner.

35. How can I store my microgreens properly before use?

Keep the microgreens in a closed container at a temperature of 38-40°F (3-5°C) preferably in a fridge. Some, like Basil, are sensitive to low temperatures and if kept in a temperature below 32°F (0°C) will change appearance to black or dark brown after a few hours.

Chapter 8

Some Microgreen Recipes

Beef Burger

Prep Time: 15 minutes

Cook Time: 10 minutes

Total Time: 25 minutes

Servings: 6

Ingredients

To make the burger:

- ½ cup microgreens of choice
- 2 lb ground beef, grass-fed
- ½ cup feta cheese, crumbled
- 1 tbsp olive oil
- 1 ½ tbsp chipotle-adobo sauce
- 6 brioche buns
- 1 tbsp butter
- Freshly ground black pepper
- 1 ½ tsp kosher salt

To make the aioli:

- ¼ tsp ground mustard
- 2 large garlic cloves
- 2 tbsp fresh lemon juice

- 1 tsp kosher salt
- ¼ cups olive oil
- 1 cup fresh mint leaves, loosely packed
- 1 ripe avocado

To make the pickled onions:

- 1 minced red onion
- ½ cups apple cider vinegar
- 1 ½ tsp kosher salt
- 1 tbsp sugar

Directions

1. Put 1 cup of water, vinegar, 1 tbsp of sugar, and 1 ½ tsp of salt in a bowl and combine. After the salt and sugar have dissolved, pour the mixture into a jar containing the red onions. Set aside at room temp. for 1 hour.
2. Get an immersion blender and add your garlic cloves, mustard, 1 tsp salt, lemon juice, ¼ cups of olive oil, mint, and avocado to its base. Set to high speed, and process until you have a smooth mix. Alternatively, you could use a food processor.
3. Now, mold the ground beef into 6 patties. They should all be 1 inch thick. Press down with your thumb to make an indentation at the center of the patties. Next, put the burgers in your fridge.
4. Heat your oven up to 350 degrees F.
5. Drizzle some of the chipotle-adobo sauce on your brioche buns. Bake them in your oven for 6 minutes.
6. Melt olive oil and butter in a large skillet placed over high heat. Take the patties from the fridge and brown them in the pan. If you want the patties medium rare, then 6 minutes of cooking should suffice.
7. After cooking all the patties, set them aside to cool.

8. Arrange the burgers in this way: bun, aioli, patty, onions, feta cheese, microgreens, and close with another bun.

Nutritional Information

Calories: 564 Total fat: 33 g Total carbs: 8.2 g Protein: 55.6 g

Parmesan and Ricotta Cheese Pizza with Microgreens

Prep Time: 1 hour

Cook Time: 18 minutes

Total Time: 1 hour 18 minutes

Servings: 4-8

Ingredients

To make the dough:

- 3 tbsp organic olive oil
- ¾ cup boiled water
- 1 tsp sea salt
- 2 ½ tsp dry active yeast
- 1 tbsp local honey
- 2 cups organic whole wheat flour

To make the toppings:

- ½ cup microgreens
- ½ cup ricotta cheese
- 4 diced smoked bacon
- ½ cup shredded parmesan cheese
- ¼ cup minced pistachios
- 2 tbsp olive oil

- ¼ tsp sea salt
- ½ tsp freshly ground pepper

Directions

1. Put yeast, water, and honey in a bowl. Combine for about 5 minutes to make the mixture frothy.
2. Next, add oil and mix some more.
3. Get a second bowl and mix salt and flour. Pour this mixture in the first bowl and, using a wooden spoon, mix some more. Set the bowl aside for the dough to swell.
4. After sitting for 45 minutes, beat the dough down and cover the bowl with a plastic wrap. Put this bowl in your refrigerator.
5. Preheat your oven to 500 degrees F.
6. Spread the dough in a pizza baking pan and sprinkle with cornmeal.
7. Get a bowl and add pepper, ricotta, salt, parmesan, and olive oil. After mixing, pour the ingredients on the pizza dough. Add diced bacon and ½ of the pistachios.
8. Put the pizza in the oven and bake for 18 minutes. You want the bacon to be brown and crispy.
9. Garnish with microgreens and ½ of the pistachios.

Nutritional Information

Calories: 229 Total fat: 10.7 g Total carbs: 27.5 g Protein: 6.1 g

Sunflower Guacamole

Prep Time: 5 minutes

Cook Time: 0 minutes

Total Time: 5 minutes

Servings: 4

Ingredients

- ½ minced jalapeno
- 2 avocados
- ¼ cup minced red onion
- ½ cup lime juice
- ⅔ cup chopped sunflower shoots
- ¼ tsp salt

Directions

1. First, add salt, avocado, and lime juice into a bowl. Mix well and add minced red onion, sunflower shoots, and jalapeno.

Nutritional Information

Calories: 191 Total fat: 15 g Total carbs: 15 g Protein: 4 g

Mini Strawberry Chocolate Tart

Prep Time: 5 minutes

Cook Time: 15 minutes

Total Time: 20 minutes

Servings: 2

Ingredients

To make the filling:

- 1.5 oz goat cheese
- 1 ½ cups strawberries
- ½ cup basil microgreens
- 1 tbsp maple syrup
- 2 tbsp Greek yogurt

To make the crust:

- ¼ cup coconut oil
- 1 cup almond flour
- 2 tbsp maple syrup
- ½ tsp salt
- 1 tbsp cocoa powder

Directions

1. Preheat your oven to 350 degrees F.
2. For the crust, get a medium bowl and whisk almond flour and salt in it. Add the oil and maple syrup to the bowl and mix to form a dough.
3. Separate the dough into two parts and press each into two small pie pans. Using a fork, make holes all over the doughs.
4. Transfer the pan to the oven and brown for about 15 minutes. After, take the pan out and let sit for a few minutes.
5. Except for the microgreens and strawberries, add every other ingredient for the filling into a blender and pulse. Spread the mixture onto your crust and add the microgreens and strawberries on top.

Nutritional Information

Calories: 797 Total Fat: 62.3 g Total Carbs: 44.1 g Protein: 21 g

Sheet Pan Fajitas with Bell Peppers and Chickpeas

Prep Time: 10 minutes

Cook Time: 20 minutes

Total Time: 30 minutes

Servings: 4

Ingredients

- Hot sauce
- 3 medium yellow bell peppers
- Fresh cilantro
- 2 cups cooked chickpeas
- 8 corn tortillas
- 1 medium yellow onion
- 3 tbsp olive oil
- ¼ tsp cumin
- 1 tbsp chili powder
- ½ tsp garlic powder
- 1 tsp fine sea salt

Directions

1. Preheat your oven to 450 degrees F. Line a baking sheet with parchment paper.
2. Mince the yellow onions and bell peppers and add them to the baking sheet. Also, add the chickpeas. Pour some oil on this mixture and sprinkle salt, chili, cumin, and garlic powder on it.
3. Toss well with clean hands and even them out.
4. Bake in the preheated oven for about 10 minutes. Take out the baking sheet, stir the ingredients, and return the pan to the oven for another 10 minutes.
5. Serve immediately with tortillas, hot sauce, and fresh cilantro.

Nutritional Information

Calories: 606 Total Fat: 18.5 g Total Carbs: 92.7 g Protein: 23.6 g

End of Summer Salad

Prep Time: 5 minutes

Cook Time: 5 minutes

Total Time: 10 minutes

Servings: 2

Ingredients

- 1 ½ tbsp mint, minced
- 3 ½ cups arugula microgreen
- 2 tbsp diced caper berries, remove the stems
- 1 cup ripe blackberries
- 1 crushed garlic clove
- 2 tbsp pine nuts
- 1 tbsp red wine vinegar
- 1 ear red corn, the cob removed
- 2 tbsp olive oil
- ½ bunch white asparagus
- Black pepper
- Sea salt

Directions

1. Rinse the arugula. Dry them and set aside.
2. Add oil, caper berries, vinegar, garlic, and mint to a small mixing bowl. Add a pinch of salt too. Mix and place the bowl in your refrigerator.
3. Cut off the ends of your asparagus, leaving the soft parts. Coat your spears with olive oil. Set your grill to medium heat and sear your asparagus. Sprinkle with salt and pepper and chop the asparagus into ½ inch pieces.
4. Get a large bowl and add the arugula, blackberries, asparagus, corn, and pine nuts. Add the salad dressing in the small bowl and serve immediately.

Nutritional Information

Calories: 265 Total Fat: 21.1 g Total Carbs: 19.7 g Protein: 5 g

Bacon Hash Brown Casserole with Eggs

Prep Time: 45 minutes

Cook Time: 35 minutes

Total Time: 1 hour 30 minutes

Servings: 6

Ingredients

- Handful minced microgreens
- 8 strips applewood smoked bacon
- 6 large eggs
- 4 cups peeled russet potatoes, grated
- Olive oil
- 1 cup yellow onion, grated
- 1 tbsp minced garlic
- 1 cup fresh breadcrumbs
- ¼ cup seeded and minced jalapeno peppers, wash and dry the peppers
- 1 ¼ tsp salt
- Freshly ground black pepper

Directions

1. Place a large saute pan over medium heat and add the bacon to it. Cook each side for 5 minutes, then take the bacon out. Place on a large plate lined with a paper towel. Don't discard the grease.
2. After grating the onions and potatoes, squeeze the liquid out of them. You want to get out as much liquid as you can, so take your time.
3. Preheat your oven to 375 degrees F.

4. Into the greasy pan, add jalapeno peppers, breadcrumbs, garlic, and the wrung out potatoes and garlic. Add olive oil, set the stove to medium-high heat, and cook for about 20 minutes. Stir occasionally. To prevent the potatoes from sticking to the bottom of the pan, you can add a bit of olive oil.
5. Crumble your bacon and put the pieces in the pan. Add salt and pepper, and stir.
6. Add the mixture in your pan to a 9x13 baking dish.
7. Press down with the back of a spoon to form an indent in the middle of the potato mixture.
8. Break your eggs into the dish, but space them out. Transfer the pan to your oven and bake for 20 minutes.
9. Finally, take the pan out of the oven and let sit for 10 minutes. Top with microgreens and serve.

Nutritional Information

Calories: 678 Total Fat: 49.2 g Total Carbs: 41.5 g Protein: 18.9 g

Microgreens with Strawberry-Lime Vinaigrette

Prep Time: 10 minutes

Cook Time: 0 minutes

Total Time: 10 minutes

Servings: 1

Ingredients

To make the salad:

- Strawberries cut in two
- 6 oz microgreens
- 2 minced radishes

- Fresh herb sprigs
- 12 minced snow peas

To make the vinaigrette:

- 3 tbsp olive oil
- 1 ½ cups chopped strawberries
- 2 tsp lime juice
- 2 tbsp white balsamic vinegar
- 1 tsp pure maple syrup

Directions

1. For the vinaigrette, add strawberries, maple syrup, and vinegar into a bowl and combine. Set aside for 30 minutes. Holding back the strawberries, pour the liquid into another small bowl. Add oil and lime juice into this second bowl and stir. Mix in salt and pepper.
2. For the salad, add the microgreens, radishes, ¼ of the vinaigrette, and snow peas into a bowl. Add the strawberries you reserved and toss. Top with sprigs and halved strawberries.

Nutritional Information

Calories: 105 Total Fat: 8 g Total Carbs: 9 g Protein: 1 g

Lemon and Pea Tendril Risotto

Prep Time: 5 minutes

Cook Time: 18 minutes

Total Time: 23 minutes

Servings: 2

Ingredients

- ¼ cup microgreens
- 3 peeled garlic cloves, minced
- 2 tbsp butter
- 2 oz pea tendrils, roughly chopped
- ⅓ cup parmesan cheese, grated
- 1 lemon
- Pinch saffron
- 1 deseeded red bell pepper, diced
- 3 tbsp vegetable demi-glace
- 1 cup bomba rice
- 1 yellow onion, peeled and diced

Directions

1. Peel the rind of the lemon and mince to get 2 tsp of zest. Seed the lemon and cut it into quarters.
2. Add 2 tsp of oil into a medium pot and place it over medium heat. Put salt, pepper, onion, and garlic into the pot and stir for 5 minutes.
3. Next, add the bell pepper and cook for 4 extra minutes.
4. Pour rice into the pot and set the heat to medium-high. Stir and cook for 2 minutes.
5. Add 3 ½ cups of water, vegetable demi-glace, lemon zest, lemon wedge juice, and saffron into the pot. Add some more salt and pepper if you wish. When the water starts to boil, turn the heat down to medium and cook for 16 minutes.
6. Turn off the heat and add butter, parmesan cheese, and the chopped tendrils.
7. Serve topped with pea tendrils, microgreens, and lemon wedges.

Nutritional Information

Calories: 198 Total Fat: 13 g Total Carbs: 18.5 g Protein: 5 g

Mediterranean Quinoa Salad

Prep Time: 5 minutes

Cook Time: 10 minutes

Total Time: 15 minutes

Servings: 2

Ingredients

For the salad:

- 2 cups microgreens
- 1 cup uncooked quinoa
- ½ chopped avocado
- 1 cup halved heirloom tomatoes
- 1 oz canned cooked black beans
- ½ cup pitted kalamata olives
- 2 ½ tbsp minced green onion

For the dressing:

- ½ cup olive oil
- 2 cloves large garlic
- ¼ cup fresh basil leaves
- ¼ cup red wine vinegar
- 1 tsp kosher salt
- 1 tsp black pepper

Directions

1. To make the dressing, put salt, basil, red wine vinegar, garlic, and pepper into a food processor. Slowly pour the oil while at high speed. Put the mixture into a bowl for later.

2. Cook quinoa according to the directions on the pack. Set aside to cool.
3. Afterward, add the remaining ingredients to the quinoa. Take the dressing out of the fridge and add 2 tbsp to the quinoa.
4. Serve immediately or store in your fridge.

Nutritional Information

Calories: 1002 Total Fat: 74.7 g Total Carbs: 72.1 g Protein: 18.9 g

Charred Rainbow Beet and Pistachio Salad

Prep Time: 10 minutes

Cook Time: 45 minutes

Total Time: 55 minutes

Servings: 2

Ingredients

- 2 small rainbow beets, scrubbed and trimmed
- Canola oil

For the basil olive oil:

- 2 cups basil, loosely packed
- 1 cup microgreens
- ¼ cup oil, scant
- 1 tbsp pistachios, chopped
- ½ cup lemon juice
- Pinch kosher salt
- Citrus herb salt

Directions

1. Place the ingredients for basil olive oil into a blender and pulse.

2. Toss the trimmed beets with 2 tsp of canola oil and place them on a baking sheet. Wrap with aluminum foil.
3. Set the grill to 350 degrees F and cook the beets for 45 minutes. Set the beets aside to cool.
4. Next, peel the skin off your beets and halve them.
5. Pour some of the basil olive oil onto 2 plates. Add ½ the microgreens and beets to each plate. Sprinkle with pistachio and herb salt. Top with what's left of the microgreens.
6. Serve immediately.

Nutritional Information

Calories: 346 Total Fat: 33.5 g Total Carbs: 14.6 g Protein: 2.5 g

Roasted Broccoli Microgreen Soup

Prep Time: 5 minutes

Cook Time: 25 minutes

Total Time: 30 minutes

Servings: 6

Ingredients

- 2 tbsp red balsamic vinaigrette
- 1 head broccoli, chopped
- 3 tbsp sunflower seeds, roasted
- 1 large minced onion
- 2 tbsp lemon juice
- 4 whole cloves garlic
- 1 cup cooked navy beans
- 1 tbsp olive oil
- 3 oz feta cheese
- 4 cups vegetable broth, low-sodium

- 1 cup sunflower shoots and 1 cup zesty mix microgreens
- ¼ salt
- ½ tsp chili powder

Directions

1. Place a rimmed baking sheet in your oven and preheat to 425 degrees F.
2. In a bowl, mix broccoli, oil, onion, salt, and garlic. Spread this mixture on your hot baking sheet and bake for 25 minutes.
3. Get a food processor and add the baked vegetables, lemon juice, broth, feta cheese, microgreens, beans, and chili powder. Pour this mixture into a saucepan and add a little water or broth. Warm the mixture.
4. Drizzle with vinaigrette and top with microgreens, cheese, and some sunflower seeds. Serve.

Nutritional Information

Calories: 309 Total Fat: 7.2 g Total Carbs: 47.2 g Protein: 15.2 g

Mushroom and Microgreen Omelet

Prep Time: 10 minutes

Cook Time: 0 minutes

Total Time: 10 minutes

Servings: 1

Ingredients

- 3 large eggs
- 1 tbsp unsalted butter
- ¾ cup microgreens
- 1 ½ oz minced white mushrooms

- Freshly ground pepper
- Coarse salt

Directions

1. Place a nonstick skillet on a stove set to medium-high heat. Melt ½ of the butter in the pan and cook the mushrooms for 2 minutes. Add salt and pepper, and stir.
2. Brown the mushrooms for 2 minutes and transfer into a small bowl. Add microgreens. Clean the skillet with paper towels.
3. Get a medium bowl and break the large eggs into it. Add salt and pepper and whisk. Put the remaining butter into the pan and melt. Cook the eggs without stirring. The omelet should set after 2 minutes, then add the cooked mushrooms and microgreens.
4. Serve immediately.

Nutritional Information

Calories: 322 Total Fat: 26.5 g Total Carbs: 2 g Protein: 19.8 g

Asparagus, Tomato, and Microgreen Salad

Prep Time: 15 minutes

Cook Time: 15 minutes

Total Time: 30 minutes

Servings: 6

Ingredients

To make the salad:

- ½ cup toasted slivered almonds
- ½ lb asparagus
- 4 cups arugula microgreens

- 2 small, diced Roma tomatoes

To make the dressing:

- 2 tbsp chopped parsley stem
- 1 medium grapefruit,
- 2 tbsp olive oil
- Pinch black pepper
- Pinch sea salt

Directions

1. Preheat your oven to 350 degrees F. Use aluminum foil to line a baking sheet. Add slivered almonds to the pan and bake for 7 minutes. Take the almonds out and set aside to cool.
2. Zest and juice the grapefruits, and add both into a small bowl. Mix and add parsley stems and oil. Whisk well and sprinkle in salt and pepper. This is the vinaigrette.
3. Boil a pot of water and cook the asparagus for 2 minutes. Take the vegetable out and keep in a bowl of ice water. Still crunchy, dry the asparagus and cut them into 1-inch pieces. Put them in a bowl and add chopped tomatoes and ½ vinaigrette. Toss.
4. Get another bowl. Add the remaining vinaigrette and microgreens. Add the asparagus mixture and serve.
5. Add toasted almonds as toppings.

Nutritional Information

Calories: 124 Total Fat: 9 g Total Carbs: 10.2 g Protein: 3.8 g

Kale and Radish Microgreen Salad

Prep Time: 10 minutes

Cook Time: 0 minutes

Total Time: 10 minutes

Servings: 2

Ingredients

- Pinch minced parsley
- Pack kale microgreens
- 1 julienned cucumber
- 1 chopped small red radish
- 1 julienned carrot
- 2 chopped small grape tomatoes
- 1 diced celery stalk

To make the dressing:

- 1 tsp lemon juice
- 2 tbsp aged balsamic vinegar
- 2 tbsp olive oil
- 1 tbsp avocado oil
- Pinch white pepper
- Pinch sea salt

Directions

1. Add the ingredients for the dressing into a small bowl and whisk thoroughly. Small balsamic balls will form in the mixture if you do this well.
2. In a 2:1 ratio, add the kale and radish microgreens on a flat plate. This ratio works well because radish has a stronger taste.
3. Place your cucumbers and carrots on the microgreens and, around the edges of these vegetables, add the slices of tomatoes, celery, and radish.
4. Sprinkle parsley and salt and drizzle with dressing over the veggies.

5. Serve.

Nutritional Information

Calories: 216 Total Fat: 15.3 g Total Carbs: 18.9 g Protein: 3.3 g

Seared Sea Scallops with Microgreen Salad

Prep Time: 5 minutes

Cook Time: 4 minutes

Total Time: 9 minutes

Servings: 4

Ingredients

- 1 tbsp olive oil
- 12 dry sea scallops
- 3 diced radishes
- 2 cups microgreen salad mix
- Freshly ground black pepper to taste
- Salt to taste

To make the miso and lime dressing:

- 1 tsp soy sauce, low-sodium
- 3 tbsp sweet white miso
- 3 tbsp fresh lime juice
- 2 tsp minced garlic
- 1 tbsp sesame oil
- 1 tbsp agave nectar

Directions

1. For the miso and lime, add soy sauce, white miso, garlic, agave, lime juice, and sesame oil into a small bowl. Pour in 3 tbsp of water and mix.
2. Cut out the still-attached side muscles of the scallops. Then, add salt and pepper to the scallops.
3. Put the microgreen mix and radishes into a different small bowl, and add 3 tbsp of the dressing. Toss and set aside. This is your salad.
4. Place a skillet over medium-high heat and pour in 1 tbsp of olive oil. Cook your scallops in the pan for 4 minutes. That's 2 minutes for each side.
5. Place the scallops on four plates and add the salad on each. Drizzle with what is left of your miso and lime dressing.
6. Serve immediately.

Nutritional Information

Calories: 201 Total Fat: 7.6 g Total Carbs: 16.3 g Protein: 17.2 g

Seared Halibut with Microgreens Salad

Prep Time: 25 minutes

Cook Time: 8 minutes

Total Time: 25 minutes

Servings: 4

Ingredients

- 6 cups assorted microgreens
- 2 peeled kiwi, chopped
- ⅓ cup torn fresh mint leaves, loosely packed
- ¼ cup chopped English cucumbers
- ⅓ cup torn fresh basil leaves, loosely packed

- 3 cups fresh strawberries, halved and minced
- ¼ tsp ground cinnamon
- 1 tbsp olive oil
- 4 6-oz halibut steaks, skin and bones removed
- Pinch ground cayenne pepper
- Pinch ground black pepper
- Pinch sea salt

Directions

1. Mix cucumber, lemon juice, kiwi, oil, strawberries, ½ salt, and black pepper into a small bowl. Let sit.
2. On every side of the halibut, rub with the remaining salt, cinnamon, black pepper, and cayenne.
3. Lightly coat a skillet with nonstick cooking spray and place the pan over medium-high heat. Cook the halibut in the skillet for 8 minutes. Turn the fish to make sure you get all sides. Turn off the heat and set the pan aside.
4. Into the strawberry mixture, mix the basil and mint.
5. Place microgreens on a plate, then add the halibut and basil mixture. Serve.

Nutritional Information

Calories: 312 Total Fat: 8 g Total Carbs: 54 g Protein: 39 g

Microgreen, Zucchini, and Carrot Cake

Prep Time: 6 minutes

Cook Time: 10 minutes

Total Time: 16 minutes

Servings: 4

Ingredients

- 1 tsp garlic powder
- 1 cup microgreens
- 2 tbsp chickpea
- 2 zucchinis
- 3 eggs
- 2 carrots
- 1 cup parmesan cheese, grated

Directions

1. Into a large bowl, shred the zucchini and carrots. Chop microgreens into the bowl and add parmesan cheese.
2. Break the eggs into a small bowl and add flour, salt, pepper, and garlic powder. Pour this into the large bowl and toss.
3. Add spoonfuls of this new mixture into an oiled sheet pan. With the back of the spoon, flatten the mixture into patties and bake for about 10 minutes. Serve.

Nutritional Information

Calories: 123 Total Fat: 5.4 g Total Carbs: 11.1 g Protein: 9.2 g

Super Microgreen Smoothie

Prep Time: 5 minutes

Cook Time: 0 minutes

Total Time: 5 minutes

Servings: 3

Ingredients

- 1 oz broccoli microgreens (kale is a good alternative)

- 1 diced banana
- 1 cup milk
- 5 large strawberries
- ¾ cups vanilla Greek yogurt
- Ice

Directions

1. Add all these ingredients into a blender and pulse until you get a smooth mixture. Serve.

Nutritional Information

Calories: 124 Total Fat: 2.5 g Total Carbs: 21.9 g Protein: 5.4 g

Blue Cheese Tomato with Microgreens

Prep Time: 10 minutes

Cook Time: 0 minutes

Total Time: 10 minutes

Servings: 4

Ingredients

- Handful microgreens
- 2 chopped, medium-sized ripe tomatoes
- 3 tbsp balsamic glaze
- ½ cup blue cheese, crumbled
- Salt and pepper to your taste

Directions

1. Place the tomato slices on a plate and sprinkle with salt, pepper, and cheese.

2. Drizzle glaze over the seasoned tomatoes and add microgreens as toppings. Serve.

Nutritional Information

Calories: 85 Total Fat: 5 g Total Carbs: 6 g Protein: 4 g

Cold Smoked Salmon Sandwiches with Microgreens

Prep Time: 15 minutes

Cook Time: 0 minutes

Total Time: 15 minutes

Servings: 4

Ingredients

- 3 small cress microgreens
- 6 slices soft wholemeal sandwich bread
- 14 minced cucumbers
- 100 g cold smoked salmon
- Butter

Direction

1. Spread butter on one side of each slice of bread.
2. Separate the microgreens, smoked salmon, and cucumber between the bread. Stack all the sandwiches together and cut them diagonally.

Nutritional Information

Calories: 140 Total Fat: 7 g Total Carbs: 21 g Protein: 8 g

Vegan Microgreen Soup

Prep Time: 5 minutes

Cook Time: 6 hours

Total Time: 6 hours 5 minutes

Servings: 4

Ingredients

- 2 carrots, chopped into small circles
- 1 tbsp olive oil
- 1 large cubed potato
- 1 medium onion, diced
- 1 tbsp dried parsley
- 2 chopped garlic cloves
- 8 oz cauliflower microgreens
- 2 chopped celery stalks
- 3 cups water
- 1 oz rum
- ½ tsp thyme
- 1 tsp salt

Directions

1. Put the oil in a pot and place it in a crock pot. If you don't have one, this soup can also be made in a coffee maker with a warming tray.
2. Cut onions, garlic, and celery into the pot. Pour rum into this mixture.
3. Add three cups of water to the crock pot and stir. If you're cooking in a coffee maker, add three cups of water and allow it to trickle through the machine, as this will heat the water up more quickly.

4. After an hour, add the microgreens and let cook for an additional hour.
5. Mix in salt and spices.
6. Add this mixture to your blender and puree until smooth.
7. Add carrots and potatoes to the pot. After cooking for 4 additional hours, serve.

Nutritional Information

Calories: 160 Total Fat: 3.5 g Total Carbs: 25 g Protein: 4 g

Conclusion

The microgreen stage is, arguably, the best time to consume vegetables. At this point in their development, the nutrient content and flavors of the greens are heightened. So, if you buy into the philosophy of eating your food as medicine, you should add microgreens to your diet.

They are also widely eaten now, so cultivating microgreens is commercially viable. Hopefully, this book has been useful in helping you successfully plant and harvest your microgreens. The materials needed to cultivate microgreens are relatively affordable and easy to set up. But the biggest incentive, some would say, is the fact that microgreens can, generally, be harvested in less than a month.

Microgreens can be used as a garnish or made into a smoothie. Refer to the recipes in this book as often as you need to for creative ideas on how to consume the greens.

References

Bliss, R. M. (2014). Specialty greens pack a nutritional punch. United States Department of Agriculture. https://agresearchmag.ars.usda.gov/2014/jan/greens

Choe, U., Yu, L. L., et al. (2018). The science behind microgreens as an exciting new food for the 21st century. *National Library of Medicine 66(44)*, 11519-11530. doi: 10.1021/acs.jafc.8b03096

Huang, H., Jiang, X., et al. (2016). Red cabbage microgreens lower circulating low-density lipoprotein (LDL), liver cholesterol, and inflammatory cytokines in mice fed a high-fat diet. *National Library of Medicine 64(48)*, 9161-9171. doi: 10.1021/acs.jafc.6b03805

Patil, B. (2016). Vegetable and fruit improvement center. Texas A&M Agrilife Research. https://vfic.tamu.edu/

Bonus!

Wouldn't it be nice to have even more motivation and inspiration on your gardening journey? As a sincere "Thank you" for reading my book, i've given you access to a FREE Indoor Gardening ebook below!

Go to This Link to Get Your Free Bonus Indoor Gardening Ebook:

bit.ly/Indoorgardeningfree

These indoor gardening tips helped me immensely with my indoor growing. I hope they help you too!

Lastly…

If you enjoy this book then I'd like to ask you for a favor. Would you be kind enough to **leave a review for this book on Amazon?**

It'd be greatly appreciated & will likely help other avid green thumbs with their projects! I read EVERY review I receive and each one helps me to serve each and every one of you better, so your feedback is highly valued!

Thank you,

Basil Green

www.ingramcontent.com/pod-product-compliance
Lightning Source LLC
Chambersburg PA
CBHW071919070526
44583CB00016B/2055